Orange and White and Tweets All Over
A Collection of Anti-Trump Poems

edited by
StarShield Lortie

A THURSTON HOWL PUBLICATIONS BOOK

Orange and White and Tweets All Over

A Thurston Howl Publications Book
Published by Thurston Howl Publications
thurstonhowlpublications.com

jonathan.thurstonhowlpub@gmail.com

Cover image by Tabsley

Edited by StarShield Lortie.

Printed in the United States of America
10 9 8 7 6 5 4 3 2 1

Contents

ORANGE AND WHITE AND TWEETS ALL OVER

Weasel

———————————————

passing through

stopped for gas at the border of mississippi
mom & pop station
where the tanks wore their dust
as badges because they survived
and still haven't retired

we walked in to pay the bill
grab ourselves a bottle of caffeine
to wake up from seeing trees, dirt, and cars
that's all there is when you're trekking
across state lines—emptiness, and the road

cashier's hands shook as she rung up
our pile of candy bars and energy drinks
and i wondered if the cracks in her hands
spread her skin like earth when it quakes

two men stood on each side of her like body guards
crumbs shuffled through their beards
as they stared us down
and while I reach for my wallet,
one leaned over,
"what's a brown boy doing this side of mississippi"

i looked over to my husband
whispered for him to wait in the car

then turned to the man, "just passing through"

his eyes searched for something inside me
as if to find any excuse to say i was lying
he brushed his denim jacket back
revealed his .45 hanging at the waist of his pants
his hand eager to pull it out
shoot me dead

i stared him down
our eyes fought
like two flames in separate fires
each flicker adding fuel
to each other's disgust

she gave me a total
i slid $25 across
raised the sleeves of my hoodie
didn't wait for the change

i wanted to tell him
to stuff his pride up his ass
and pull the trigger

he wanted to be a man
beat his chest with his gun
and say he killed the brown boy
because it's people like me
who make america suffer

J. D. Morrison

_____

Trump Haiku

Stormy Daniels
One-hundred-thirty-thousand
dollars . . . bigly spent.

James Penha

2020

My lover Mohammed and I had joined
husband to husband in Niagara Falls
six years before but after our right
to marry was nullified I removed my
mother's miraculous medal from around
my neck and signed up for the Registry
together with Mohammed so of course
we couldn't vote yesterday but at least
we had a home in which to watch Wolf
project the President had lost. Mohammed
and I embraced but within the hour the
tweets began—FALSE, FAKE NEWS,
RIGGED—we saw the army move in
on CNN and the times I see
now will never be the same.

Jelliqal Belle

Tricky Dick Limerick

There once was a man named Trump
who liked to on everyone dump
'til he was caught bare
dancing in flaming underwear
then people laughed at the chump

6

Tyson West

The Problem with Monsters

We cherish monsters – they are fun to watch
our risk is knowing not when they will bite.
Against the backdrop of hate and white fright
he struts at rallies, and warbles his crotch,
a weird comb over hiding his bald splotch.
He blames the poor and blacks to mint his might
we cherish monsters – they demand we watch,
our risk is knowing not who they will bite.
What saves our asses is this boy will botch
the easiest decision just to spite
the chief he follows who stood cool and bright,
whose deeds and words glow clearly as top notch.
We cherish monsters – we want wrecks to watch.

Sam Dutton

Bring on the Clown

Bring on the clown!
Bring on the clown!
His sleazy smile white
upon tan orange-brown.

He enters the ring
to the jeers of the crowd;
a minority cheer him
equally loud.

He leers at the women
then closes his mouth
about gun legislation.
He ignores the kids' shouts.

He targets minorities
and those who came
to live the dream
as it now slowly fades.

But don't you worry
there's a painful equality
as he targets low incomes
for the vast majority.

Roll out the cannons

to the 'yes' peoples' cries,
his hand over red
despite protestors' cries.

Kaboom!
is the sound
as he presses down,
leaving ticker tape lives
strewn on the ground.

The Earth's clap is thunderous;
a pained roared response
to the nightmare devastation
that could knock at our doors.

Most of humanity gasps
at the farce playing out,
shouting 'Stop this insanity;
Remove this clown now.'

NightEyes DaySpring

Except...

America is the land of the free,
> except when you are working for the man,

and the home of the brave,
> except if you are a homeless vet.

A nation that extends rights to all its citizens,
> except when that conflicts with someone else's
> freedom of religion.

Here you can worship however you choose,
> except if you are Muslim,

and engage in life,
> except if someone decides to use you as target
> practice,

liberty,
> except if you are an illegal immigrant, gay, trans,
> Black, Hispanic, Native American, or not a
> White, straight male, then some restrictions may
> apply,

and the pursuit of happiness,
> except we're constructing a society that forces
> people to take on debts they can never hope to
> pay back for their education and health care.

A land of opportunity and promise,
> except if you are poor.

A land of peace and prosperity,
> except for our endless wars.

A land with liberty and justice for all,
> except of course for you.

Jelliqal Belle

Ode to Change

Build a wall
fiery hall
stick my dick up her pussy to my balls.

Paid her off so she won't grouse
as I move to the White House.
Kick out bad hombres that arouse

distrust,
only lust,
money, power, thrust, thrust, thrust.

I have a plan
from that Banner man
but I am not a pawn of the klan.

Sometimes you tear down
to build greatness from the ground
believes the orange headed clown.

Only I have vision
is the blind man's provision
I pray we survive this democratic collision.

Fake news and lies
hackers try,

let not America die,

For this will pass
like the 70's crisis for gas,
maybe our next president won't be an ass.

Tyson West

All the Best

Baby, we can debate all night
whether all the best cowboys have Chinese eyes
but no one questions that
all the best despots are voids
that the vacuums of their wills struggle to fill.
Just this last century Joe the man of steel,
after poisoning Lenin and ice axing Trotsky,
packed the Georgian steppes of Joe's emptiness with
wisps of thirty million starving souls.
Adolph checked out – raging against the fools who
            followed him,
singing the sad old country song
how he poisoned his dog and suicided his wife
while the Russians repo'd his pickup.
Thank our founding fathers who set us up to get served
            only despot lite.
Donny the fat bully, our bone spur commander in chief,
rises with all the panache and morals
of a drug dealer with dementia –
so high and tweaking he can't recall his own lies.
Our world and myths need be much softer – for this is
            where we eat and sleep,
my teen twins with their partners du jour
chatter so wisely foolish at my squeeze and I across the
Olive Garden table.
Dreaming of elite universities that will reject them

but ready to settle onto safety net cow college campuses
where they will have their ignorant insecurities abraded
            away
and become snared in the candy crush of student debt.
The Honduran waitress smiles to fluff her tip
as we twirl our pastas in the simpatico glow of corporate
            consistency.
Some smiling basketball star

or country singer will tweedle that we are all family which
we will believe because love, even the fake stuff, is the
            coziest quilt.

Donnie in his dark web will swirl in his bowl of tweets and
fire his way through bureaucrats, lieutenants, and flunkies
            who laugh behind his back
then leak his secret servile slather of Putin.
Yet our lives will go on
this chaos and incompetence
will go off the air if not get cancelled mid-season.
Our children will have children
with no idea that their lives are harder
so long as smart phones message them on Facebook
and the Olive Garden keeps our blood sugars
at levels where all is well.
A new leader will appear on the air
to entertain us
and most of us will be there
debating all the best.

Marcus Awoolius

The Wall

Build that, Build that, Build that wall.
Build it, Build it, Build it tall.
Build that, Build that, Build that wall.
Build it, Build it, Build it tall.

An issue heeded
by a nation
with solutions needed,
to problems seeded
by drug war.

Reefer madness turned to quarter ounces,
Legalisation, a response to federal pounces
on users and pushers,
filling up prisons ,
for another kind of pusher.

In our cities,
Drug War gives way,
to Gang War.
Gears of war,
Oiled with money and blood.

Lives wrecked.
Families wrecked.
Communities wrecked.

Cities wrecked.
Countries wrecked.

So build the wall,
The wall so tall.
The wall which will end all
of the strife in
America's heart.

Up in My Wherever

maybe a dollar fraction is in there
like the worth of more than virginal slut-hood
and yeah maybe I like being on my knees
but only to those deserving of all of me
submission must be earned
not arroganted
maybe my right to speak
to think
to be different
without being attacked
is that hiding up in there
and in some countries
girls sit out school
without the cotton
to bandage up a monthly bleed
that here we'd rather perfume
and regulate to perfectly timed packeting
and a curricula of denial and lies
educating gender roles
and tired tropes of only prescribed pressuring and
resistance
and sex as a scored game of predator and prey
school board certified fan fiction
rather than science
factioning pundit prejudice over fact
because it's easier to draw on caricature than complexity
even when it's deadly

our reality is a marketed edited infotained and
infotainted Hawthorne effect hell
of bleached spray-tanning waxing grandiose
visibility reserved for the loud in deed, word, and volume
while pain and passing are insignificant statistics
assaulted numbers
without dollar signs
without enough digital spacing to count
maybe my value is in there
my values untraditionally married to a desire for equality
maybe my personhood is incorporated up in there
up in my most independent defiant blood
still waiting to come out from   shhh ...
from
up in
my wherever

Deborah Chava Singer

All I Want for Not-Actually-My-Holiday-Christmas

I want everyone going around expressing how grateful they are that they now get to say "Merry Christmas" to quit with that bull because we all know they used to go around every winter holiday season saying it anyway and then complain about not getting to say it when they just did and both of these ways of talking about Christmas are basically equally annoying.

I want it to be appropriate for me to send angry emails to my family that voted for Bigly Orange Hateball every time he does something messed up but who has that kind of time and I'm not talking to them anyway because I had some maturity epiphany and decided I didn't need to keep being around people who tell me I'm going to Hell, make my dignity a doormat, and/or make me feel bad.

I want the friends and family I'm still talking to, to not have to be so afraid for all the different reasons we've been made afraid for the last two years.

I want the media to learn from their mistakes and get better. I want to not hear about polls or polling data or what the polls are predicting ever again!!!

I want people to realize that while wanting the right

to live free from prejudice and discrimination and
wanting the right to be prejudiced and to discriminate
are competing interests, they are not equally competing
interests. They are not at all the same type of thing.

I want an intelligent president, who is thoughtful and
reasonable, who appreciates the gravity of the role
they've been given. I want a president who is respectful
of all Americans, including undocumented ones, and
seeks to bring us together as a country where we are all
valued as human beings.

However, since that is, sadly, apparently too much to ask,
I want President Hateball to drop his smartphone in his
toilet while he's tweeting. And I want there to be video.

Deborah Chava Singer

Trump's the President and I Can't Figure Out if I'm Depressed

the world has gone crazy
everyone's mad
and here I am, mentally ill,
with every trick, skill and hack
I've learned for managing
being put to the test
like never before
bigly
trying to decipher
yet again
grief from depression
symptoms from electoral side effects
fear from anxiety
pissed off rage from irritability
shocked disbelief from numbness
the desire to avoid people
who possibly hate
or just carelessly damned
me, mine, and nearly everyone else
from an episodic inclination for withdrawal
and maybe all this I'm feeling
all this I'm gripping and gritting
grappling and reeling
every wave of heartbroken sorrow
terror and despair

is only another go from the thing
I've been weathering for years
each new distracted brain swirl
I'm been slogging and crawling through
just more of the usual
or maybe too much really is too cruel
asking myself again
is reality real
because that means different strategies
of how to deal
I'm tired and I'm angry
and I don't want to make nice
and unify
I want to pout
I don't want to talk
I want to yell
and I want to nothing at all
maybe it is just my depression
acting up again
but this time it has a cause

Tyson West

Black Paintings

Can fear, our guilt, and self-hate have a face?
Or do we spread them around like Goya's
black paintings wrapping the walls of his space
where id and ego birth paranoias?
We craft conspiracies to half believe
then fester as we lose our cushy jobs
and self-respect. In such depths we perceive
bad hombres coming at us like lynch mobs.
A hero will appear to save our world
whose wall will stop dark skinned men and Islam
as porn star dalliances come unfurled
pale preachers will forgive him with a psalm
once we elect this conman as our head
he gaslights us into the walking dead.

Tyson West

We Let Him In

We let him in, the troll who leads us now
like drunken Uncle Joe, who acts highbrow
at first, his racial slurs seem just a joke.
A border wall is something James K. Polk
would build to keep out blood thirsty Mau-Mau.

My white pals pretend his business know how
will save us. Secretly they hope he'll plow
the black man's efforts under in one stroke
we let him in?

This flabby bully boasts he won't allow
our deep state weakling diplomats to bow
to dirty dictators or colored folk
what spine he claims he had goes up like smoke
as he kneels to lick Putin's footsies – Wow!
We let him in.

Jonathan W. Thurston

A Sonnet for a Blue Bird

To see a man sitting behind his desk
and know his job is Commander-in-Chief:
this scene becomes a portrait so grotesque
for you will not enjoy any relief.
to see him pet his blue, blue bird and grin
while we, the people of the nation, weep
and dream of days when we were great back when,
when rainbows trumped hashtags and—bless Meryl Streep!
to watch the news and sit and wonder why
the Fox raiding the henhouse of our state
is saying that the blacks and gays should die,
and that the Russia thing's not a debate.
            Orange and white and tweets all over, right?
            He's with his bird #inplainestfuckingsight.

CONTRIBUTOR BIOS

MARCUS AWOOLIUS: What time he doesn't spend
working, Marcus Awoolius spends reading, playing
video games, and pursuing his lifelong interest in
writing. After all, when you keep coming back to it,
that means something. He is currently writing a book
titled *Contractors*, which stars a young vulpine named
Kaylatetketten from a race known as the Kemmar who is
the apprentice of an older Human Bounty Hunter named
Esau. It's what occupies the bulk of his creative time and
he hopes to have the first rough draft completed by the
end of 2018.

JELLIQAL BELLE: Jelliqal Belle builds new worlds as
she is unsatisfied with this one. Animals don't talk, cars
don't fly, and no one has magic. She strongly believes
this is an editorial error that needs to be corrected
at the first opportunity. Jelliqal writes fantasy with
a suspense twist. From her small office window, she
watches the sunset in Metro Atlanta, GA. She has an
indulgent husband, a collegiate son, and impatient pets.
Jelliqal is often teaching others the craft and confidence
of writing. Art is not for the weak hearted. Jelliqal is
the writing facilitator of Furry Weekend Atlanta. She
has had numerous short stories and poems selected for
publication. Tales from Jelliqal Belle can be found in
Roar8 and the upcoming publications THP's Breeds:
Foxes and Furplanet's Dissident Signals. The author
is also a contributor to Werewolves Versus in their
Hollywood and Fascism e-book anthologies and will
be in the 780 page print edition of Werewolves Versus:

Volume One, expected Summer 2018. @Jelliqal on Twitter, Telegram, and Slack.

NIGHTEYES DAYSPRING: NightEyes DaySpring is a known troublemaker who is rumored to have a penchant for coffee and an interest in dead, ancient civilizations. He has been actively writing furry fiction since 2010. His stories have appeared in *Werewolves vs. Fascism, Seven Deadly Sins,* and *FANG,* along with other anthologies. He also co-edited *Dissident Signals*, an anthology of dystopian furry literature. Currently, NightEyes resides in Florida with his boyfriend, where in his spare time he masquerades as an IT professional. For updates on his writing, visit nighteyes-dayspring.com, and for day-to-day nonsense, follow @wolfwithcoffee on Twitter.

SAM DUTTON: Sam Dutton is a writer and nature lover who lives on the edge of Dartmoor National Park in the South West of England. An avid reader of fiction and poetry, she has a Bachelor of Arts (Hons) degree in English Literature. Her writing credits to date are: 'Wolf: A Short Story.' in *Wolf Warriors: The National Wolfwatcher Coalition Charity Anthology* (2014) Thurston Howl Publishing, 'Fairytale Wonderland.' in *Wolf Warriors: Winter Wolves* (2016) Thurston Howl Publishing, 'Sweet Child of Nine' in *Poems To My Younger Self* (2018) Compiled and edited by Sarah Michelle Lynch.

J. D. MORRISON: J.D. Morrison is the author of *27 AD* @ All Things That Matter Press, *THE WAY IT REALLY IS* @ City Lights Press, and *GARY* (coming soon) @ Thurston Howl Publications. He has a bachelor's degree from the University of Maryland and master's degree from Syracuse University, both in engineering. His semi-nomadic wanderings include living in six different states and fifteen different homes. Besides writing, he enjoys playing guitar, spinning and achieving his obligatory 10,000 steps per day. He is married to his muse and editor, Jena. Together they have five children and two grandchildren. He lives in northern Virginia with his wife and two cats, Black and Decker.

JAMES PENHA: A native New Yorker, James Penha has lived for the past quarter-century in Indonesia. Nominated for Pushcart Prizes in fiction and poetry, his LGBTQ+ stories appear in the 2017 and 2018 anthologies of both the Saints & Sinners Literary Festival and the Seattle Erotic Arts Festival. His essay "It's Been a Long Time Coming" was featured in *The New York Times* "Modern Love" column in April 2016. Penha edits *TheNewVerse.News*, an online journal of current-events poetry. @JamesPenh̲a̲

DEBORAH CHAVA SINGER: Deborah Chava Singer is originally from San Diego, California where she studied truth with the Mesa College Theatre Company and Queer Players. While going to school (in something else) in Toronto, Ontario she remembered what she really wanted most was to be a writer. She currently resides in Vancouver, Washington. Her writing has appeared in *Lemondead Food Zine* from Chicken Milkshake Zines, *Santa Fe Literary Review*, *The Human Touch*, *Cirque*, *Fear and Ruin* from Pidgeonholes, *MUSE*, *Jonathan*, *Chaffin*, *Heart and Mind Zine*, *Snapdragon*, *Twisted Vine*, *Labletter*,

Off the Rocks 18: An Anthology of GLBT Writing, Rockhurst Review, Trajectory and *Steam Ticket*. In 2012 she received a GAP grant from Artist Trust to work on her play *Hidden Potential, or The Straight Gene*.

JONATHAN W. THURSTON: Jonathan W. Thurston is an editor for Weasel Press and a reporter for Michigan state LGBT paper, *Between the Lines*. His novellas *The Devil Has a Black Dog* and *Straight Men* were published in 2018.

WEASEL: Weasel is a degenerate author and The dude of Weasel Press. His latest chapbook of poems, *We Don't Make It Out Alive*, was published in May of 2018.

TYSON WEST: Tyson West, born in Boston, MA, traveled all over the East during his childhood. He largely grew up in Greenville Pennsylvania with its unspeakable beautiful post office, and attended the University of Virginia, the University of California, and New York University. He is a father and a writer and active in real estate. Much of his inspiration comes from dealing with families and estate property. Tyson West currently lives in Eastern Washington with its beautiful vistas, dry dusty summers and cold winters on the bottom of the channeled scablands of the great Ice Age flood. He enjoys reciting his poetry to magpies and coyotes. He has published fiction, form poetry, free verse and micro poetry. He is on the Haiku Registry and a member of the Furry Writers Guild.

www.ingramcontent.com/pod-product-compliance
Lightning Source LLC
Chambersburg PA
CBHW031637040426
42452CB00007B/854